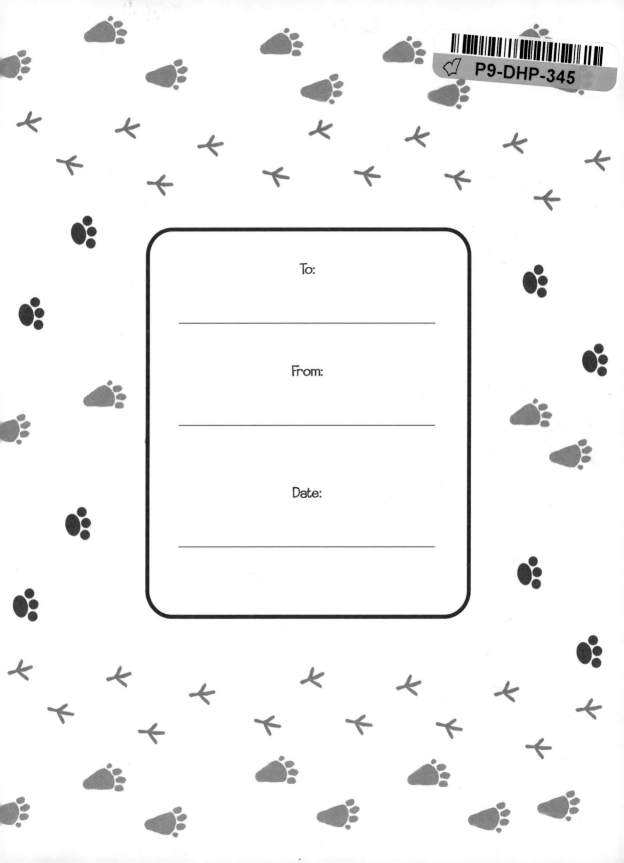

P9-DHP-345

To:

_____

From:

_____

Date:

_____

NOAH'S NOTEBOOK

How God Saved Me, My Family, and the Animals from the Flood

Allia Zobel Nolan

Illustrated by Linda Clearwater

HARVEST HOUSE PUBLISHERS

EUGENE, OREGON

Noah's Notebook

Text Copyright © 2009 by Allia Zobel Nolan
Art Copyright © 2009 by Linda Clearwater

Published by Harvest House Publishers
Eugene, Oregon 97402
www.harvesthousepublishers.com

ISBN 978-0-7369-2508-2

Original illustrations by Linda Clearwater. Regarding the art in this book, you may contact Linda at lindaclearwater.com

Design and production by Mary pat Design, Westport, Connecticut

Printed in China

09 10 11 12 13 14 15 /IM/ 10 9 8 7 6 5 4 3 2 1

For God, who has blessed me with the greatest gift: the ability to write and share His Word with others; for my dad, Alvin, whose sense of humor I inherited; for my husband, Desmond, whose belief in me gives me constant joy, and whose love I marvel at daily; for Mary pat Pino, my friend and creative director extraordinaire; and for Jean Christen at Harvest House, for her patience, friendship, and guidance in bringing this book to young and old alike.

Allia Zobel Nolan

For my parents, who have been my "ark" on several occasions, and my daughters, Genevieve and Danielle, who continually remind me of life's endless miracles.

Linda Clearwater

Dear Friends,

A long, long time ago…and I mean a long, long time ago, when I was a child and first heard the story of Noah, I absolutely loved it. To me, Noah was a great adventurer, going where no man has gone before.

I really enjoyed reading about Noah and his love for God, a bond so strong that Noah gave up his way of life, built a huge boat (and wound up the joke of the neighborhood), and sailed off on a sea of rain with no idea of where he was going and what would happen to him.

All Noah knew was that God said He would protect him. And that was enough. Noah was definitely not a worrier. He was…and is…my hero.

That's why I wrote this book…to celebrate Noah and his great adventure of faith. I have tried to put myself in his sandals, and I hope I have uncovered a side of him you may not have thought about.

I also hope this book reminds you that, though some rain will fall into your life, our loving God is always with you and will always protect you. Remember, too, to love and trust God with all your heart…because, like Noah, you never know where He is taking you.

Blessings and joy,

Allia Zobel Nolan

ENTRY #1

Haven't told a soul—not even my wife—about this yet. But God talked to me today. Honest. I was standing in my garden, minding my own business, when I hear this voice. It's not like you could mistake it. It was God, all right. And boy, was He upset.

He says to me, "Noah, I'm very disappointed. The people I made have turned out awful—present company excluded, of course. They've totally forgotten about Me. And they're doing bad things, which as you can imagine, does not make Me happy."

Me, listening to God

Hatool, my cat

Now, the hair on the back of my neck stands up straight, and my hands begin to sweat.

"I'm really sorry, God," I say. "Is there anything I can do?"

"As a matter of fact, there is," God says. "But first, I have some bad news and some good news."

I gulp and get ready for the worst.

"Well," God continues, "there's no easy way to say this. I'm sad about it, but I'm starting over. I'm sending some rain. It will wipe out everything."

"And the good news, God?" I ask Him.

"The good news, Noah, is that you and your family will be safe. I will protect you. I promise," God says.

"Now, get a notebook. Here's what I want you to do."

The neighbors, Zeb and Ari, fighting and cheating each other, as usual

ENTRY #2

"Ready, Lord," I say, and God tells me, "Sit down, Noah. This will take a while."
So I do.

"I want you to build a boat," God says. "Not just any boat—a great, big, wide boat. So think big, Noah. Think two-football-fields long. Think ARK!"

My eye is starting to twitch. Handyman of the year, I'm not. The last time I used a hammer, I broke two thumbs and a toe. While I'm thinking, *What's an ark?* God reads my thoughts.

"Don't worry, Noah," He says. "Your sons can help you."

Okay, now I'm *really* worried. Wonderful boys, Shem, Ham, and Japheth, but ship-builders they're not—especially Ham. All he thinks of is breakfast, lunch, and dinner.

"Trust me," God says. "And listen, Noah. Gopher wood."

"Okay, Lord, but where do I go?" I ask.

My sons, Shem, Ham, and Japheth

Gopher wood

"No, Noah. That's the *kind* of wood you'll need."

"Yes, Lord," I say with a red face. "Any idea how much?"

"I'm getting to that," God replies, and in one breath He gives me the details.

"The ark should be 450 feet long, 75 feet wide, and 45 feet high. You'll need a roof, a door, and a window. Make three levels: lower, middle, and upper. That's how much wood you'll need," God says. "Got that?"

MORE ENTRY #2

I'm no math wiz, so I reply the only way I can.

"A lot of wood, God." I tell Him. "We're going to need a lot of wood."

"And some pitch to coat the ark inside and out," God says. "This boat has to float."

"I'll bring some bubblegum in case we get leaks," I add.

"Good idea," God replies.

"Anything else, Lord?"

"Food," says God. "Take every kind of food you can get your hands on."

A bucket of pitch

Clean

So I'm thinking to myself, *Even Ham couldn't finish off that much,* when God says...

"Now, about the animals..."

"Animals?" I ask, gulping. "Where will I get them, Lord?"

"They'll come to you," God says. "Take seven of every clean animal, and two of all kinds of unclean animals, and..."

"What? There's more?" I interrupt. "Remember, Lord? I have allergies."

"...birds and all kinds of creatures that crawl on the ground."

I guess my face sort of gave me away.

"Trust Me," God says. "Everything will be fine. Just trust Me."

Birds

Unclean

Creepy crawlies

11

ENTRY #3

Well, the news about the ark is out, and everyone thinks I'm either sick or crazy.

"Too many spices in the lamb stew last night," my wife says when I tell her we have to build a big boat. "You have indigestion. That's all."

"But..."

My darling wife

"So you'll eat a plain diet for a while," she says. "You'll get more sleep. In a week you'll forget this."

My sons think I'm losing it too.

"Dad," they said this morning, "you've lived in a tent for all these years. Why the boat now?"

"Because I'm the patriarch, and I say so," I tell them.

I finally broke down this afternoon and let them all know WHO wants the boat. I'm not too sure they believed me. But, just in case, they are putting a bit more effort into their work. The boys' wives still have doubts. I can tell. And the neighbors can't stop making fun of me.

The boys and me building the boat

"Does Noah know-ah something we don't?" Jacob the sandal maker teased me.

"Always trying to outdo me, huh, Noah?" said Solomon the blacksmith, joining in. "I have one son—you have three. I have twenty sheep—you have fifty. I build a toy boat—you build a cruise ship. Where will it end Noah—this keeping up with the Titelbaums?"

Their jokes are very annoying. But I tell my wife, "Don't listen. Trust God. We've got work to do."

She rolls her eyes.

The neighbors laughing

13

ENTRY #4

This is the first time I've
had a chance to write in ages.
But what great news I have! We're finished, finally.
It only took us a hundred years. I'm no artist, but
here's what the boat looks like...
Not bad, huh?

The ark...
FINISHED

The wives had a bit of a shock today, though. While the boys and I were out buying more wheat, the women stayed on deck rearranging barrels, puffing out pillows, and making sure we had enough air fresheners. All of a sudden, the ground starts to shake.

"Don't look now," Shem's wife tells her mother-in-law, "but two elephants, two water buffalo, a couple of camels, and some giraffes are coming this way."

Spiders, on their way to the boat

And, as if that weren't bad enough, she says, "Oh, and how cute. Look, two spiders are walking behind them."

My wife screams to high heaven: "SPIDERS!" Then she runs away and hides behind some bags of barley. You should have heard the uproar when I got home.

"A FEW animals, you told me. Some cats, a few dogs, MAYBE an elephant," she yells. "YOU NEVER SAID ANYTHING ABOUT SPIDERS!"

"Don't worry," I reassure her. "They can bunk in Ham's room."

ENTRY #5

And that was just the beginning. Before long, all kinds of animals are hopping, jumping, flying, skipping, prancing, crawling, waddling, and storming onto the boat.

You never heard such a racket! Hisses, roars, twittering—and that was just from the wives. The noise from the animals was even worse. Moos and baas; oinks and squeaks; woofs, howls, and meows. I couldn't hear myself think.

The animals
God sent

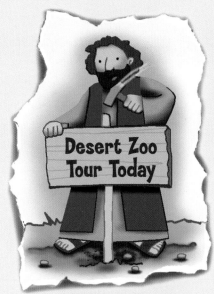

Teitelbaum putting up a sign

And can you believe it? My neighbor, Titelbaum, started bringing people around on tours. He's charging them to see our boat! He calls it *Noah's Folly: The One and Only Desert Zoo.*

But we finished loading the food today. And God spoke to me again.

"It's time now, Noah," God says. "Take your family and go into the boat. Stay there until I tell you to come out." As usual, my wife was angrier than a spitting llama. Wednesdays she takes belly dancing at the Bedouins' tent.

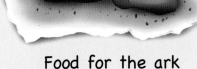

Food for the ark

"What? Two hours," she says to me. "I'll only be two hours."

Drip, drop, drip, drop. Suddenly, we hear rain on the roof.

Then *BANG!* Without warning, God shuts the door. And the rain comes down harder.

"Look," I say to my wife, "I'll buy you ten more sessions as soon as we get back."

ENTRY #6

Tonight was scary, though, I have to admit. The rain was pounding on the roof, and I was praying I had put enough sticky goop on the boat's bottom so that we don't sink. But then I remembered what God told me. *Don't worry. You'll be safe. I'll take care of you, I promise.* So I swallow my fear and put my faith in Him.

Still, I say to my wife, "Don't look out the window." But she does anyway.

"What's to see?" she asks, pulling a face. "It's just water."

I look out and there was water, all right. There was so much water it looked like an ocean...though, come to think of it, I've never seen an ocean. But if I had, I'm sure it would look like that. All of a sudden, I felt something like a huge hand give us a push, and then the boat started moving.

"I hope you bought travel insurance," my wife says, and then in the same breath she orders me out of the kitchen. "Can you do something about the smell?" she calls over her shoulder.

"I'll try," I say. But it's not as if I can crack open a window. Anyway, I went down below to see exactly how bad the smell was. Let's just say it was very bad. That's when it hit me: *We need a poop deck.*

Okay, so I'm trying to figure out how we can do this when the wife calls me for dinner. So I go back to the kitchen, but nobody's around. Then the whole family jumps out at me. *They're throwing me overboard,* I thought. But it was worse. They started singing:

HAPPY BIRTHDAY TO YOU!
YOU'RE GOD'S FAVORITE HEBREW.
MAY YOU LIVE 'TIL 1000
NOAH, WE ALL LOVE YOU!

It took me a while to blow out all 600 candles. By then the whole family was asleep. So I ate a piece of honey cake. "Happy birthday, Noah," I said to myself.

My 600th birthday cake

ENTRY #7

Bad weather blew in all of a sudden. ZAP went the lightning. KABOOM went the thunder. The rain lashed down and the wind rocked the boat.

"I'm a little nervous, God," I whisper, "not to mention seasick." Soon as the words were out of my mouth, I get a flash-back of God speaking to me again. *Don't worry,*

The lightning ZAPPING
The thunder KABOOMING

Noah. Trust Me. So I do. Meantime, the whole family's greener than the alligators on deck 2.

"See what you can do about those animals," my wife says. "Sounds like a zoo down there."

I go below and give the animals a little pep talk.

"Listen up, now," I say, trying to calm them. "I know you're all scared and upset, but God sent you here for a reason. And believe me, being here on the ark is a *good* thing. It might be rough going for a while, but God will see us through. He promised He'd keep us all safe. And I believe Him. You should too.

"What's more, while you're here I want us all to be

friends. Lions, no eating the lambs. Birds, leave the worms alone. Frogs, keep your tongues away from those flies."

"Neigh," said a horse in agreement.

"Any questions?" There were none. So I said, "Listen, I don't know how long we'll be traveling. But as soon as I know, you'll know."

It must have been a good speech. Two monkeys clapped. So did a walrus, and the horse stamped his foot three times. Then they all quieted down.

Animals clapping after my speech

ENTRY #8

Every day I look out at the sky. It's the same thing: rain, rain, rain.

And every day, I look over at my wife. It's the same thing: nag, nag, nag. I don't know what's worse.

"Are we there yet? When will the rain stop?" she asks about a hundred times a day. And each time, I give her the same answer.

"God only knows, dear," I say truthfully.

"Yes, I know HE knows, but do YOU know?" she asks impatiently.

"Dear," I say time after time, "we'll be there soon. So why not just enjoy the trip?"

"ENJOY THE TRIP?" she yells at the top of her lungs. "It's been raining for 40 days and nights. I'm cooped up with zillions of animals eating and doing their business, and my husband says he talks to God but can't even ask Him which way we're headed..."

She pauses and then smoothes down her dress. "Where are we going anyway?" she asks in a much lower voice.

"God only knows," I tell her yet again, and she rolls her eyes.

"I just hope He hasn't forgotten us."

"God wouldn't do that," I tell her. "Be patient."

No sooner are the words out of my mouth when we hear this really loud *CLUNK*. And the boat stops.

The ark hitting a mountain

"See? Didn't I tell you?" I ask, and then I put on the biggest smile ever.

MORE ENTRY #8

Okay, then we hear a scream that would clean out a year's worth of earwax. It was Japheth's wife. I thought something had bit her. So the wife and I run upstairs.

"What is it?" we ask her.

"It's the sssssssss-uuuu-nnnn!" she stutters.

"The what?"

Then I notice it's really bright. I look at the window, and there are streams of sunlight coming in.

It's the sun, all right. I look up to heaven. "Thank You, Lord," I say. "I knew You'd keep Your promise."

Then everybody starts hugging everybody. And I couldn't help myself. I turn to the wife.

"What did I tell you?" I say to her, taking her hands and swinging her around. "Didn't I say we'd be here soon?"

"Yes, and you were right," she admits in a low voice.

"Japheth, mark that down. After 577 years of marriage, your mother finally said I was right about something. Praise the Lord!"

The wife and me dancing in the sun

This got a really big laugh, even from the wife, and then the whole family joined in. We sang and danced in circles. What a great day!

When I recovered, I went below to let the animals know. A seal was playing spin-the-turtle on his nose. A beaver was brushing his teeth, and two monkeys were sitting and reading between the lions.

"I've got great news, guys," I say, and they all turn my way. "The sun is out!"

Me, telling the animals the rain has stopped

ENTRY #9

It's been very windy lately, and the water seems to be drying up. The mood on board is 100 percent better. Everyone is super anxious to get off the boat, but we're not going anywhere until God says so. In the meantime, I had an idea.

"I need a volunteer for a scouting mission," I say. Every hand, wing, and paw in the place goes up. I choose the raven.

He high-fives all his friends and then takes off out the window. But he flies back in an hour. So I know we're not out of the water yet.

Me, sending a raven to find land

I send a dove next. Same thing happens. But she doesn't take no for an answer. She keeps pestering me, so I let her try again. This time, she brings back an olive branch. Things are looking up.

I wait another seven days, and send the dove out again. This time, she doesn't come back. And today my wife says

The dove, with an olive branch

she thought she saw green grass.

"Noah, I think it's Ireland," she says. "We landed in Ireland. Hurry up. Let's get off and see the leprechauns."

"Leprechauns, shleprechauns," I tell her. "We'll leave when we're told."

God must have been listening, because...

"You can come out now, Noah," God says. "Bring your family and the animals."

Well, as you can imagine, there was an immediate stampede, and within minutes, every ant, cockroach, panther, panda, and penguin, not to mention rhinoceros and yes, even the spiders, made a beeline for the door. I moved out of the way just in time.

MORE ENTRY #9

I must say I was a bit disappointed. Only a few animals stopped to wave goodbye. My wife tried handing out comment cards that read: "Scratch here if you: enjoyed your trip, liked the service, would travel with us again." But most of the animals bolted before she could get to them.

It was heaven being on earth again, and as soon as I felt the grass under my sandals, I dropped to my knees.

"Lord, I praise You," I prayed. "You said You'd keep us safe. And You kept Your promise. How can I ever thank You?"

Then, one by one, my family knelt and gave thanks as well. Suddenly, we hear this loud shrieking. I open my eyes to see two monkeys jumping excitedly and pointing up. I look and see streams of color—purple, blue, green, yellow, orange, and red—in the sky.

Monkeys pointing to the rainbow

"It's a rainbow, Noah," God says. "I've put it in the sky for a reason. It's the sign of an agreement I make with you and all living creatures. Never again will I destroy the world with a flood."

"Thank You, Lord," I say, relieved, as at my age I don't think I could pull off another long-distance journey.

"And Noah," God says, "you did a good job. So I'm going to bless you and your family, and give you all the earth. Enjoy it, and take care of it."

So we did. The wife was thrilled. She picked some prime waterfront real estate, and we pitched a tent. I listened to the wonderful silence and fell asleep for a week.

Me, dreaming of God laughing

I got up today, though, and the wife says, "Maybe we should build a nice boat to use on the lake. What do you think, Noah?"

This time, I rolled *my* eyes. Then I went back to sleep. And guess what? I dreamt I saw God laughing.

THE END

GLOSSARY

A
ark—a big boat or a ship.

B
Bedouin—a group of people who roam the desert and live in tents.

C
cooped up—to keep closed up/in a tight space/place.

F
folly—something that is very silly or foolish.

G
gopher wood—a strong type of wood Noah used to build the ark. No one knows for certain exactly what tree or plant it came from.

H
Hebrew—the name given to God's chosen people who were also called Israelites.

honey cake—a cake made of spices and honey.

P
pitch—sticky pine tree juice that Noah used to seal the ark and make it waterproof.

S
stampede—a rush of animals running all together.

T
trust—to believe in with all your heart.

STUFF YOU MAY NOT *KNOW-A* ABOUT NOAH

Betcha' Didn't Know...

God didn't invent rain until He created man (Genesis 2:5). So how did plants get water? Streams bubbled up from the earth and watered everything. Neat. No one knows for sure, but some people believe there was no rain at all until the time of the flood. No wonder folks thought Noah was bonkers.

Noah had a good, long life. When he was 500 years old, he became the father to Shem, Ham, and Japheth. He took his world tour on the ark when he was 600. He lived until he was 950 years old, and there was no more room to put candles on his cake.

The ark took approximately 100 years to build.

Something to Laugh About...

Ned: What instructions did Noah give his sons about fishing off the ark?

Ted: I don't know.

Ned: He said, "Go easy on the bait, boys. I only have two worms."

Then God blessed Noah
and his sons,
saying to them,
"Be fruitful and increase
in number and fill the earth."

GENESIS 9:1